Miss Olen Barrett

March 1945

TIME IMPORTUNED

By the same Author

Stories

MR. FORTUNE'S MAGGOT
LOLLY WILLOWES

Poems

THE ESPALIER

TIME
IMPORTUNED

☆

SYLVIA TOWNSEND
WARNER

CHATTO & WINDUS : LONDON

1928

PRINTED IN GREAT BRITAIN
BY T. AND A. CONSTABLE LTD.
AT THE UNIVERSITY PRESS
EDINBURGH

PR
6045
, A812
TS
1928

103629

To

VICTOR BUTLER

CONTENTS

viii

TIME
IMPORTUNED

☆

THE ARRIVAL

WHEN I set out I did not know
Whether an ash tree or an elm
With branches waving slow
And a soft summer voice would overwhelm
My questing thoughts with the certainty of arrival ;

But now on the dusky lawn I stand
And neither ash nor elm tree greet :
A deeper plumage is fanned,
The air wanders enchanted with one sweet,
And in the lime tree a nightingale is singing.

THE LOAD OF FERN

Now I am sure
That the year is come to the turn, though Summer delay,
Sitting drowsily in the mute shade of the sycamore,
Waiting for moonrise, for one last moonrise more
To pour its floating silver over the stooks
That kneel all night and pray,
Motionless, like saints in heaven who kneel and adore ;
Yes, now I am sure, though Summer delay, her dear,
Her last looks taking, her looks of leave-taking,
That the year is come to the turn ;
For lumbering down from the moor
The farm carts creak and sway with their load of fern,
With their load of fern, a wilder load than hay.

So thunder-still is the air
That while they are yet far off I can hear
The axles whine and the horses snort,
And the long ring of shouted speech,
As solemnly wain follows wain, and each in turn
Delays awhile, shifting with slow care
Under that bronze bulk, under that vast rustling and toppling freight,
To steer true through the gate.
And now they plough
Onward through meadow grasses that cleave and cling
To spokes and felloes

As ripples cleave dividing about the prow
Of the ship who comes slowly, slowly into port.
Steady she keeps on her way, and her sail bellies
As near she passes and nearer, and you can hear
Her canvas thud and her blocks complain, men's voices, and the ring
Of chains and winches and pulleys and all her gear,
Till for love of her, unknown, and unknown her seafaring,
The heart stands up to cheer her.

O now I think how the year
With all her freight of harvest, with all her gear
Of seed and blossom, of berry and bracken frond,
Puts into port.
But here she cannot stay :
She must put forth again, she must away,
Steer for the equinox, hold out her sail
Taut to the buffeting wind, wince under hail,
On, on, into the winter seas that lie beyond,
Into the deep nights, into the sheer
Darkness, into fog and storm and snow,
Into the grinding frost, into the shortest day . . .
O the long voyaging ere she can return
With her load of fern !

But you, last freight, and emblem of the close,
Last-garnered, furthest-fetched, and most her own,
Sweet breath of the wild, harvest untended and unsown,
Tawny with long regards of the sun on solitude,

3

Wise-rooted, nurtured with natural sap alone,
Strong gipsy child of an earth virgin and unsubdued,
Come in and house
Your warmth and scent of summer, come in, come in !
Here in a drowsy twilight roofed with stone
Store your sweet breath with cattle breathing warm
Sweet sighs of quietude, espouse
To indoor dusk your rust and russet glows,
Bring warmth, scent, colour, bring the wild earth's well-being into
    shelter ;
Ere the first trumpet of the gale be blown, or the storm
Beat like a distant drummer, or Winter begin,
When the winds arouse and the rains pelt
And helter-skelter the leaves scud off from the groaning boughs.

SHORT sleep, brief waking,
Dawn like a bird flown by,
The swollen sun forsaking
His dark bower of cloud
And sinking beneath the mountain ;
My slender rill of time
Still bubbling from the fountain
With voice not loud,
But loud enough to chime
Me to my meditations ;
Years making and unmaking
The net of constellations ;
Winter, a look of rime,
And Spring, a blossom falling,
And Summer, a blade of corn,
Soon ripened, soon bowed ;
These, Lord, with patience
I glean, and wait thy cry,
Thy word recalling
Me from these fields where I
Am, even as Ruth, forlorn.

Long sleep, eternal waking . . .

DARKENED the hedge, and dimmed the wold,
We sang then as we trudged along.
The heart grown hot, the heart grown cold,
Are simple things in a song.

The lover comes, the lover goes,
On the same drooping interval,
Easy as from the ripened rose
The loosened petals fall.

Between one stanza and the next
A heart's unprospered hopes are sighed
To death as lovely and unvexed
As 'twere a swan that died.

Alas, my dear, Farewell 's a word
Pleasant to sing but ill to say,
And Hope a vermin that dies hard ;
As you will find, one day.

SEXTON AND PARSON

'Sir, what shall we do?
Here's Edward Buckland found dead,
Edward Buckland the gipsy man,
And Paradice his wife is dead too;
Both dead of fever in their caravan.
They must have died before the storm began,
For the wind has blown open the door,
And the snow lies drifted on the floor
With never a footprint thereon.'

'What shall we do, sexton, what shall we do?—
We will bury them together, the two
In the one deep grave shall lie together,
Safe put away from their journeying, from storm and winter weather.'

'Sir, what shall we do then?
I will dig them a nice grave;
But after I shall be put to shame,
With register before me and vestry pen
And nothing to write but death and a wayfaring name—
Neither age nor walk in life nor whence they came.
As I live, Sir, the proverb is just:
In hoar-frost and gipsies put no trust,
For come noontide they are gone.'

7

'What shall we do then, sexton, do then ?—
We will enter their names in the book, and when
They died, and *Travellers* we will call them :
Travellers they, ay, and all men till sweet rest befall them.'

COUNTRY MEASURES

'THAT tune, child, which swayed you and buoyed out your frills
Till you looked like a blossom that wafts to the ground
Must have come a long journey, thus to set twirling round
The shepherds and nymphs of the Vauxhall quadrilles.

'To such country measures the haymaker swings
His scythe as he paces the meadow alone ;
As though to their requiem are the tall grasses mown,
And the moon rises over the wood as he sings.

'The traveller hears him, and pays him a sigh
(Or 'tis paid to the *lacrimae rerum*, maybe) ;
For these airs have a voice of such lorn sincerity
That the soul must assent ere the reason knows why.

'Young Careless has one that would make the tears start,
Of a girl that 's deserted and grieves for her case :
'Twas sung by a milkmaid down on his father's place,
And before he forsook her he 'd got it by heart.'

WILLOW

CATKINS, by village folk
'Tis called, and after, palm ;
Whose pewter fur rose-flushed
Sprays gold-dust and smells balm ;

Lovely on countryside—
First hatched of all the brood
Spring mothers on the brown
Nest of the English wood ;

And lovely in London too,
A greeting seeming beyond all
That envoy flowers have brought
Authentic and personal

(As we, should one beloved
Offer a keepsake, choose
No rarity but what 's most
Made his by wont to use) ;

For man has untaught the flowers
Their first obedience,
But in a willow branch
There can be no pretence.

9

I with such word of Spring
By the old brown man was plied,
Who with slouched hat, and stick,
And tousled and sad-eyed

Dog at his slow heels,
Wanders through streets and squares,
With kingcups sometimes, or groundsel,
Or russet wild pears.

Said I, close to my breath
Holding the willow wands :
' In sheltered woodlands now,
Or growing beside ponds,

There must be boughs a-plenty
With their catkins putting out.'
And as I spoke I was glad ;
For it seemed beyond doubt

That Spring, the swallow, was come,
And that under her sky
All men would be happy, though none
Should taste such joy as I.

Me narrow-hearted, how
His honest answer chid !
' Yes, it 's too common now
To fetch the price it did.'

THE MORTAL MAID

As a fish swimming through the water's glimmer
I wooed you first,
When to the wishing well you stooped your visage
And slaked your thirst.

With a hair plundered from the white beard of Merlin
You shall be tied ;
With a grass ring plighted you shall come at nightfall
To be my bride.

The straight rain falling shall be the church walls,
And you shall pace
To where an old sheep waits like a hedge-priest
In a hollow place.

In his inheritance of the kingdom of Elfin
Your son shall be born,
And you shall christen him in the dew that glistens
On the holy thorn.

THE HOUSE GROWN SILENT

AFTER he had gone the wind rose,
Buffeting the house and rumbling in the chimney,
And I thought : It will roar against him like a lion
As onward he goes.

Seven miles before him, all told—
Chilled will be the lips I kissed so warm at parting,
Kissed in vain ; for he 's forth into the wind, and kisses
Won't keep out the cold.

Closer should I have kissed, fondlier prayed :
Pleasant is the room in the wakeful firelight,
And within is the bed, arrayed with peace and safety.
Would he had stayed !

THE ESPOUSAL

Such silence was on the woods and on the meadows where none
Walked save the departing sun,
Where nothing breathed save the warm sweet of midsummers past
In quiet hayrick housed fast,
That I thought : Perhaps for no other end was I born
Than with step deliberate and unaware
To wander my way to this wood-encompassed pasture where
Stands one ash tree, all green and lorn.

Long while in silence as by a friend I sat by the tree,
Whose shadow moving over me
And lovingly lengthening such sheltering joy shed into my soul
That ere I turned homeward, its bole,
Large and austere, I twined my arm's half-hoop to embrace,
And laid my eyelids and my lips along
Its braided weather-silky bark, and looked up into the throng
Of boughs as looking up into a husband's face.

I⊤ had grown late
And I had turned inland
When one with rolling gait
Came down toward the strand :
It was a drownèd sailor.

' Greeting, poor ghost !
I do not fear you much.
On this cruel coast
There must be many such
Wandering, could we but see them.

' And wander well you may
On such a night as this,
When the smell of mown hay
Comes like a kiss
From the earth, our quiet mother.'

' Greeting, my kind
Lass-alive,' said he.
' Turn back if you 've a mind
To come walking with me ;
For 'tis seaward I 'm going.'

' Seaward, sailor ?   No !
Elsewhere let us rove.
But half an hour ago
I was down in the cove :
There is nothing there, nothing—

' Only the endless chide
Of waves furled and unfurled ;
Only a making tide,
And an ebbing world.'
' Ay, is the tide making ?

' 'Tis even as I guessed ;
For where I lay underground
Something troubled my rest,
A tremor and a sound
Under the green fields travelling ;

' Coming nearer and more near,
And searching me out
Till at last 'twas so clear
That with a great shout
I remembered, and came forth.'

' Remembered ?   Ah, poor soul,
Have you remembered all—
The ship past control,
In the icy squall
Like a maimed beast struggling ;

15

' Rearing at every shock,
Blind in blinding night,
And hounded toward the rock
By the unchanging spite
Of the sea, man's old enemy ?

' Turn back, my friend,
Turn inland once more.
At the voyage end
'Tis best to sleep ashore,
In a safe bed, and a holy ;

' Or should you wakeful lie
You need not be dismayed,
For resting near by
Are many of your trade
Who have gone down into deep waters :

' Kind company for you,
Who the long night long
Shall tell old yarns through,
And roar out the old songs,
With *Adieu to you, Spanish Ladies !* '

But he as I spoke thus
Brushed by me, with the Nay !
Of one whose imperious
Need can brook no delay ;
And in a moment, vanished.

THE RIVER OUSE

THROUGH his broad lands the river goes,
Rolling and plentiful as they ;
The willow blossom he bears away
And bears away the winter snows.

Anon to the darkening bridge he comes
And heaves his shoulder against the piers ;
His own full voice is all he hears,
He does not hear the noise of drums,

The soldiers marching overhead
For sea and foreign service bound—
High in the air a martial sound,
A passage athwart his passage shed.

On flows the river and on go they ;
Left ! Left ! drums the heart in my bosom.
More sad than snow, more dear than blossom,
My peace of mind they bear away.

I followed the river in my pain
And heard him say, secure and grave :
The tears you shed upon the wave
No tide shall ever bring again.

While yet upon your visage shine
And scald their tracks, while yet in me
You wring your hands, they haste to be
Absolved into a larger brine :

Therein, a nameless salt, they 'll weigh
The flood that bears to distant shores
Lovers as dearly lost as yours,
Or sting an unkissed cheek with spray.

You will not know, and though you should
(Since strangers these) you would not care
How they commerce with your despair—
Launch on your tears, it does you good,

Weep to encounters chance shall bid—
By then this grief may seem as strange :
Let sorrow in the water range,
Be sighs in air forever hid.

Others, more rash than you, leap down—
With every tear, with every breath,
You shred your moment's self to death :
My dear, what need is there to drown ?

IN THE VALLEY

On this first evening of April
Things look wintry still :
Not a leaf on the tree,
Not a cloud in the sky,
Only a young moon high above the clear green west
And a few stars by and by.

Yet Spring inhabits round like a spirit.
I am sure of it
By the swoon on the sense,
By the dazzle on the eye,
By the long, long sigh that traverses my breast
And yet no reason why.

O lovely Quiet, am I never to be blest ?
Time, even now you haste.
Between the lamb's bleat and the ewe's reply
A star has come into the sky.

A PATTERN OF TIME

STILL in the shining garden
Where once in time long gone
I walked alone, a maiden,
A maiden walks alone.

She halts before a rosebush
As though she could not tell
What thoughts now press upon her—
I know her thoughts full well.

Red, red are the roses ;
But yet there is something more ;
And through the garden she wanders
As though she would implore

Blossom or leaf to reveal it ;
They are silent every one :
I, only I, could tell her
What she shall tell to none.

But rapt and heedless walks she,
And furtive I hurry by ;
For it would spoil her dreaming
To look on such as I.

ELIZABETH

' ELIZABETH the Beloved '—
So much says the stone,
That is all with weather defaced,
With moss overgrown.

But if to husband or child,
Brother or sire, most dear
Is past deciphering ;
This only is clear :

That once she was beloved,
Was Elizabeth,
And is now beloved no longer,
If it be not of Death.

THE RED DRESS

DRESS, you are braver than I.
Red in grain, you 'll not fade
Though you shall be laid
In an oak chest, by and by.

Others shall lift you thence
To the patter and stir
Of shrivelled lavender,
With female reverence

Murmuring in awed tone :
' So rare the web, so rich
The broiderer's stitch on stitch,
See, it will stand alone ! '

Good dress, I charge you, be
In other time, other place,
To some woman of my race
True as you were to me.

In the warfare of sex
Be at eye's onset
Like the ring of a trumpet,
To challenge and perplex ;

When souls clash in the fray,
To the breast at stake a shield
Whose scarlet shall not yield
Nor leak of blood betray ;

And in that hour surprising
When the heart's garrison
Know themselves undone,
A flag still flying.

THE REQUIEM

WALK cautiously round Love
Who thrown and spent lies here ;
Raise not your voice above
A whisper lest he hear you—
Hush, for fear !

Rouse not those furious plumes
Whose wrath so far and fast
Pursued you to these glooms,
That have from everlasting
Waited to cast

Their shadow on this end :
This demi-god in dust,
This dust that could contend,
And a slave's courage mustered
Up for that thrust—

Not to Love's heart (that, none
Can pierce) but to his own ;
Which violence being done,
The victor stands up lonely,
And Love lies prone.

Look not too long on him
(Speak soft, and warily tread)
Lest viewing him harmless dim
Your memory of him dreadful ;
Lift not that head,

Seek not that hidden face,
Lest dying should restore
Those looks of childish grace
Which in Love's innocent morning
First Love wore.

THE JET CHANDELIER

SUNSET, sunrise,
Are but surmise ;
All change of changing days is safely hid,
And light sifts through the laurel screen,
Mute and submarine.

Here comes no wind to stir,
No sun to fade :
Here in this northward-facing room
Is a sure shade
For one who is afraid.

No colour at all
On hanging or wall—
And slowly in unshaken fires consume
The candles rising tier on tier
In the jet chandelier.

Here comes no hope to hound,
No love to smite :
Only a midnight sun illumes
This world as white
As snow, as still as night.

TRIUMPHS OF SENSIBILITY

I

ABOVE my own distress I hear
Outcry of anguish, groans of fear,
As though the trees in yonder wood
Mourned for some vegetable good.

Foul thought !   Creation's innocents,
Them but the rainy wind torments.
What, do you wail still ?   O, it 's true !
Man, the Sick Beast, has been with you.

TRIUMPHS OF SENSIBILITY

II

There is a fiend called Hug Me Tight
Who watches round me day and night.
Waxing and waning like a coal
His eyes look darkness into my soul.

I hear his loud and casual tread
Stalk through the disinhabited
House of my mind where he alone
Goes up and down, goes up and down.

He shoots no bolt, he turns no key,
He lets me sleep in the scullery ;
Of my left ear he 's made a trap
To catch the drips from the water-tap.

I am not chained, I am not tied,
But lest I run on suicide,
Or harm myself in my self-rage,
He keeps me in a glassy cage.

Sometimes my friends and lovers come
Like trippers to the Aquarium ;
They peer, they tap upon the pane,
And presently they 're gone again.

I know they are alive, because
I see their breath besmirch the glass ;
But be it sigh or be it scoff
It takes the same time to fade off.

And I am glad when they are gone ;
For Hug Me Tight will come anon,
And all their looks and all their sighs
Dismember and anatomise

Till they as I are cold and vile,
Guttering friendship to beguile
An itch of self-complacency.
Only my fiend is true to me ;

Only my fiend with supple tongue
Can lick my brain and heal the wrong
Which loving much and thinking more
Have wrought in fibres of one-score.

And then night comes, and he and I
Together in one darkness lie.
He holds me in a close embrace
And bites off my nose to spite my face.

III

' TIGER strolling at my side,
Why have you unbound the zone
Of your individual pride ?
Why so meek did you come sneaking
After me as I walked alone ?

' Since the goat and since the deer
Wait the shattering death you wield
In a constancy of fear,
By your stripes, my strange disciple,
Am I also to be healed ? '

' Woman, it was your tender heart
Did my bloody heart compel.
Master-mistress of my art,
Past my wit of wrath your pity,
Ruthless and inexorable.

' I hunt flesh by fallible sense ;
You a more exquisite prey pursue
With a finer prescience,
And lap up another's unhappiness :
Woman, let me learn of you.'

AT THE MID HOUR OF NIGHT

BETWEEN twelve and one,
Between one and two,
While I sit here alone
As I often do,

With a resolved rhyme,
With an emptied glass,
At the nadir of time
Strange things come to pass.

Many fantastic shapes
Before me detail—
A brown garland of apes,
An Indian with a flail,

A fair woman clad
In rustling shocks of corn,
An aeronaut run mad,
A little unicorn

That sings shrill and clear
With a trembling throat,
A man who flees in fear
Holding an artichoke,

A priest wearing a mask,
Tumbling acrobats,
A negress with a basket
Of avadavats—

They troop by me then,
But nothing say to me ;
These dreams of sleeping men
Which waking I see.

SAD GREEN

THE glass falls lower,
And lowers the wet sky,
And by a fire sit I
Hearing the lawn-mower

Nearing and waning—
Howbeit out of tune
The essential voice of June,
Patient and uncomplaining ;

For though by frost and thunder
Summer be overthrown,
The grass plat must be mown
And the daisies kept under.

KILL JOY

I watched the lambs at play
Within a meadow ;
And watched there, too, a grey
Unhappy wolf that lay
Still as a shadow.

As though to lure him in
The lambs were prancing :
He slobbered at the chin,
And said that only sin
Could come of dancing.

Thus saying, he nearer crept
On his empty stomach ;
Marked his bright spoil, and leapt—
O, like a love-adept
How he could mammock !

'Thwart his shag breast the slender
Booty brandished,
Off loped the greyfoot then,
And crunched it in his den
With howls of anguish.

But back he came anon
To his old covert,
Still lank, still woe-begone ;
And still the lambs played on,
Careless as ever.

' Wolf !   Wolf !   His sleep is a sham.
Fell he 'll awaken.
And will you dance till he cram
You all ? '   Said the youngest lamb :
' Friend, you 're mistaken.

' Foul looks the creature wears ;
Evil you deem him ;
Yet with our lily airs
From all his craft and cares
We will redeem him ;

' For much he longs to play
But dares not venture,
And wearier every day
Grows of his tasteless prey
And his mate the vulture ;

' So hither must he creep,
And suffer hunger,
Till with one surpassing leap
He jump in among the sheep,
And be wolf no longer.

35

' Then from all bonds of right
And wrong unfettered,
He 'll dance with us in white
Array till at fall of night
Wat, our good shepherd,

' Come, and the tale being told
Of our full number,
With joy he shall behold,
And latch us in the fold
Of innocent slumber.'

COUNTRY THOUGHT

IDBURY bells are ringing,
And Westcote has just begun,
And down in the valley
Ring the bells of Bledington.

To hear all these church bells
Ring-ringing together—
Chiming so pleasantly,
As if nothing were the matter—

The notion might come
To some religious thinker
That the Lord God Almighty
Is a travelling tinker,

Who sits retired
In some grassy shade,
With a pipe—a clay one—
And plies his trade,

A-tinkling and a-tinkering
To mend up the souls
That weekday wickedness
Has worn into holes :

And yet there is not
One Tinker, but Three—
One at Westcote, One at Bledington,
And One at Idbury.

THE DEAR GIRL

' PRETTY, say when
You will have tied your posies ?
Pinks for the men,
And for the maids, moss-roses.'

' I 've told my score ;
And yet I would apparel
One posy more
For leave-take and nonpareil ;

' And when 'tis done
I will myself bestow it
On the breast of one
To whom I think I owe it :

38

' A quiet breast,
Which nothing now amazes,
Wearing a fancy vest
Of green sprigged o'er with daisies.

' Yes, 'tis for Dick ;
I never had a fellow
With head so thick,
Nor curls so crisp and yellow.

' He sued in vain ;
I counselled him with laughter
To end his pain
With a rope's-end and a rafter ;

' And in despair
He perished at my bidding.
He too must wear
A breast-knot at my wedding.'

THE RIVAL

THE farmer's wife looked out of the dairy :
She saw her husband in the yard ;
She said : ' A woman's lot is hard,
The chimney smokes, the churn 's contrary.'
    She said :
' I of all women am the most ill-starred.

' Five sons I 've borne and seven daughters,
And the last of them is on my knee.
Finer children you could not see.
Twelve times I 've put my neck in the halter :
    You 'd think
So much might knit my husband's love to me.

' But no ! Though I should serve him double
He keeps another love outdoors,
Who thieves his strength, who drains his stores,
Who haunts his mind with fret and trouble ;
    I pray
God's curse might light on such expensive whores.

' I am grown old before my season,
Weather and care have worn me down ;
Each year delves deeper in my frown,

I 've lost my shape, and for good reason ;
    But she
Yearly puts on young looks like an Easter gown.

' And year by year she has betrayed him
With blight and mildew, rain and drought,
Smut, scab, and murrain, all the rout ;
But he forgets the tricks she 's played him
    When first
The fields give a good smell and the leaves put out.

' Ay, come the Spring, and the gulls keening,
Over her strumpet lap he 'll ride,
Watching those wasteful fields and wide,
Where the darkened tilth will soon be greening,
    With looks
Fond and severe, as looks the groom on bride.'

THE SAD SHEPHERD

OF a day's motoring, of half England left behind,
Why should this one sight be so clear in my mind ?
A country churchyard crowded with tombs and trees,
And three or four foot reared by the deaths of centuries,
So that we from the road could view as on a stage
The congregation coming out after morning prayer.
With loitering alacrity they trooped out into the air,
Greeting and grouping anew, glad to disengage
Voice and limb from decorum of Sunday demean,
Content to be going home, and content to have been.
But privily along a pathway narrow and overgrown
With hooding cypress the priest went walking alone,
Counter to the sun hastening, and away from his kind :
A black gown he wore and carried a book,
And I thought : There works some torment in that man's mind
Which he would hide from all, but which I by chance have seen—
For his lips were pinched close, and frenzy was in his look.

SONG

SHE has left me, my pretty,
Like a fleeting of apple-blows
She has left her loving husband,
And who she has gone to
The Lord only knows.

She has left me, my pretty,
A needle in a shirt,
Her pink flannelette bedgown,
And a pair of pattens
Caked over with dirt.

I care not for the pattens,
Let 'em lie in the mould ;
But the pretty pink bedgown
Will comfort my lumbago
When midnights are cold ;

And the shirt, I will wear it,
And the needle may bide.
Let it prick, let it rankle,
Let my flesh remember
How she lay against my side !

SATURDAY EVENING

'Who's he that went by just then
In a glory of speed, in Hosanna of dust,
Riding his motor-bike as though he must?'
'He? That was Ben,
One of the village young men,
Off to the town in spite of our Member's strictures,
To buy some fags, and pick up a girl, and go to the pictures.

'Well-informed Sir, you are wrong.
I do not impeach your knowledge of local
Gothic, but let me tell you how that same yokel
Was the heart of song;
And at his passage a throng
Of warriors blown from Troy to an English shire
Rose up to whirl after him, to hang on the air and admire.

EPITAPHS

I, AN unwedded wandering dame
For quiet into the country came.
Here, hailed it ; but did not foretell
I 'd stay so long and rest so well.

*

I, RICHARD KENT, beneath these stones
Sheltered my old and trembling bones ;
But my best manhood, quick and brave,
Lies buried in another grave.

*

HER grieving parents cradled here
Ann Monk, a gracious child and dear.
Lord, let this epitaph suffice :
Early to Bed and Early to Rise.

*

WITHIN this narrow cell is hived
The sweetness, wedded but unwived,
Of Mary Grove, whose loss I rue.
And here our babes lie buried too.

*

I, SARAH DELABOLE, espied
My daughter's daughter's child a bride.
They value yet my hard-won gear,
My lore not so, and that lies here.

*

As you are now so once was I,
And loved in churchyard nooks to pry ;
But bolder sports would choose, I trow,
Were I again as you are now.

POTEMKIN'S FANCY

I SALUTE thee, great Catherine,
With a strange device.
See how imperiously the torches shine
Through the walls of ice !

Steep are those walls, and thick,
And glister like tears.
Each with a torch, a seven-foot candlestick,
Stand the tall grenadiers.

Icicles are not more rigid
Than these stand to attention,
Nor heart of empress and statesman more frigid
Than this pleasure-house of my invention.

Within are the singers and trumpets,
Venice masquers and French wine,
The fairest virgins and the noblest strumpets
Of old Rurik's line,

And the English ambassador at sixes and sevens
How to sleep through such pomp :
Without is the wolfish gaze of the freezing heavens
And the frozen swamp.

Brandish your flambeaux, great Catherine !
Let all Europe admire
A palace hewn out of winter as from a mine
And streaming with fire.

But the clear walls stand fast :
They melt not, neither do we,
Inexorably bewintered in the blast
Of a measureless ennui.

ALLEGRA

' Child, it is late in the day and late in the year
For you to be lingering here.
Cold airs creep out of the churchyard clay,
The sun has gone down, the elms look hollow and sere :
This is no time, this is no place for play.'

' O, but I 'm happy here, I play as I please ;
And my companions are these
Tall stones and yew bushes, whence I peer
At the old brown man who grumbling upon his knees
Tends the hillocks, not recking a child is near.'

' But, dear, the daylight grows narrow, 'tis time you were sped
With warmth and kisses to bed ;
For now are all good children of Harrow
Asleep save you, O truant, still stirring the dead
Leaves with your footfall, swift and light as a sparrow.'

' Alas, don't send me to bed, for I sleep alone,
Not daring to weep lest my own
Uncomforted voice be a thing to dread ;
For my nursery walls are built of the echoing stone,
And cold is all underfoot, and dark overhead.'

Thus steadfast still to the same wild story clung she :
' I am always alone, for he,
The Boy who comes here, can't join in my game.
Look, yonder is where he comes, to the stone by the tree.
I pity him much, poor boy ! because he is lame.

' There with a book lies he, or else he will raise
His handsome head, and gaze
Out over the plain with a look made free
At the westering sun, and the elm-tops afloat in the haze
Like shadowy islands remote in a golden sea.'

'The body is embarked . . . I wish it to be buried in Harrow
Church.   There is a spot in the churchyard, near the footpath, on
the brow of the hill looking towards Windsor, and a tomb under a
large tree . . . where I used to sit for hours and hours when a boy.'
                              Byron to Murray, May 26, 1822.

THE PATRIARCHS

HERE might he crop the sweetest grass and here
Be cooled by sweetest airs and here by right
Of those majestic horns which year by year
In solemn increase chronicled his reign

Might none resort but he : here he withdrew,
As to his setting draws the unquestioned sun,
Kingly enough to reign in private too.
Beneath him all his realm of pasture spread :

Unhasting flowed the river, and arrayed
In noon and summer both the land had peace.
All this his yellow eyes largely surveyed,
And mounting to his ears familiar notes,

Piece-meal ejaculations of content,
Told where his happy subjects to and fro
Strayed on the lower slopes.   Up the ascent
Two strangers came, an old man and a boy.

No shadow of disquiet crossed his mind ;
By smell and gait and garb he knew they were
But shepherds, human adjuncts of his kind.
They neared, and sat them down upon the sward.

50

Their voices lulled him ; he began to doze,
For he was ancient, kingly cares he bore,
And his long day of power approached its close.
Calmly, as on the ripened landscape, he

O'erlooked the present prospect of past life :
Lordship by wax and wane of moons full-globed,
Rivals out-matched, vanquished cabals, the strife
Of fronts and the first challenge, and the ewes

Obeissant, and the warm fleece of his dam.
Forgotten fears of the wolf thronged up.   He awoke—
A voice struck on his hearing : Lo, a ram
Caught in a thicket !   By his spreading horns,

Token of sovereignty, he was betrayed.
Snorting and stamping his forehoof he stood
With brows entangled while the hawking blade
Flashed in the sun above the substitute.

In deep midnight of a deep
Midwinter's night I lay asleep,
And dream-awakened, seemed to be
Turning over drowsily
Pages brittle, brown, and sere
As leaves blown into the new year.
Such a book it was as shrewd
Sir Thomas Browne by lamplight chewed ;
Mumbling marvels, point-device
In the *Sic et Non* of lies,
And with bright clear-obscure of youth
Enchanting what it had of sooth.
But lullabied by tales that are,
Being fabulous, most familiar,
I read unheeding, and only this
Recall :
      In India there is
A vale sequestered and serene
As that momentary green
Secluded in the breaking wave.
The aspen branch a Brahman gave
To Alexander, that with cold
And lisping leafy voice foretold
To him his ending, was, men say,
Out of this valley fetched away.

There may the parent trees be found
Whose roots, deep-questing underground,
Bathe in the river of the dead ;
Thence are they always green, thence fed
With knowledge of all ends to come ;
To them the young Phoenix flies, and dumb
With awe he folds his wing, and stays
To hear, through lapse of timeless days,
Their solemn converse, calm and slow,
Reverberate death's wave below.
Hither by mountain passes grooved
Where but the eagle's shadow moved
I, to discover if a frond
Yet grew those lifeless crags beyond,
Vocal from the prophetic root,
Came unattended and on foot.
All night long the vale I roved,
Seeing through mango turrets groved
Planets and constellations rise,
Pitiless as serpent's eyes ;
And many a branch plucked I and pled
With it to learn if I were led
So many dangerous continents through,
Here to make end, with but the dew
To anoint me for my burial
Beneath the tamarind blossom's fall.
Dumb were they, till the wind of morn
Gave them a murmuring voice forlorn,

Deepening round me as the day
Flowed down the hillside, sad and grey
As water flowing.   On fared I,
Still seeking, though I knew not why ;
For nought was here for me to find
Save a green valley that resigned
Itself unto a sunless sky . . .
And then a thing of light flew by ;
So hued, and sang so clear, it seemed
A rainbow sang or music gleamed.
Not in vain had I come, not wholly
False the tale of something holy
Inhabiting among the wood ;
Since here with ravished heart I stood
And watched the Phoenix, burd-alone,
Building his pyre upon a stone.

Thither in his beak brought he
Branches of the sandal tree,
And tear-shaped golden gums he pried
From the wounded, hoary side
Of balsam-pine and benjamin.
Swift he wrought, as though within
His breast he felt the implicit flame
Quicken, a force that overcame
All bird-like dalliance and delay ;
By his own wing-strokes fanned halfway

Already to a thing of fire,
Deft and devout to frame his pyre
As that would be to undo it.   Yet
New fire, true bird, were so well-met
In him that the conjunction showed
Only how warm a bird's heart glowed ;
For having brought a bough and twined
It in the texture to his mind,
Perched on the stone, with innocent pride
He would cock his head a-side
To contemplate his work, and sing
Softly to himself, as Spring
It were, and he a nest did build.
Thus did he labour, and thus filled
With wonder I stood and watched him there,
Whilst all around watched too : the air,
Dedicate to his next flight, held
Its breath, the bubbling fountain welled
Like incense, and the woods as still
As woods in water hung, until
Having woven in some two or three
Long weeds of gleaming laurel he
Perched once more upon the stone,
And looked, and saw that all was done.
Then, then, he clapped his wings, and sang
So loud that all the valley rang,
Re-echoing his lonely joy ;
So clear, his singing seemed to buoy

The heavens up, so thrillingly
That one by one each ancient tree
Lit up with blossom, flowed with sound,
And trembling like a merry-go-round,
Slowly with majestic yearning,
Turning, turning, turning, turning,
By that loudest lay absolved,
Slowly with solemn joy revolved.

Sweet ! Sweet ! O, sweet
Death is a lovely feat
For the rash self-consumed
Who in wide air entombed
Wander forever free.
Joy ! O Joy, to be
Unwinged, so that I fly,
Disvoiced, that chant may I !
Though fine songs are sung
Flame has a shriller tongue,
And paints upon the wind
Thought's quickness unconfined.
All achievements claim
Their apotheosis of flame :
Tall towers burn higher,
Troy lives in a fire.
Time can never quench
Troy burned for a wench ;

That smoke has unfurled
A banner over the world,
And many a bright spark
Flying through Time's dark
Shall kindle the unreckoned
Host of the unquickened ;
Yea, continents yet drowned
Beneath Ocean's bound
Shall raise their heads to behold
Troy burning as of old.

Thus did he sing ; and at the word
Burning a mightier plumage whirred
Invisible, and smote the pyre,
And the air was shaken with fire.

THE TREE UNLEAVED

Day after day melts by, so hushed is the season,
So crystal the mornings are, the evenings so wrapped in haze,
That we do not notice the passage of the days ;
But coming in at the gate to-night I looked up for some reason,
    And saw overhead Time's theft ;
For behold, not a leaf was left on the tree near by.

So it may chance, the passage of days abetting
My heedless assumption of life, my hands so careless to hold,
That glancing round I shall find myself grown old,
Forgotten my hopes and schemes, my friends forgotten and forgetting ;
    But all I can think of now
Is the pattern of leafless boughs on the windless sky.

SONG FROM A MASQUE

UNDER these chestnuts and these elms
Shade is a kind of nunnery ;
And here the elder nurses sit,
And tell their tale, and rock their prams,
And wind their wool and sew their hems.

They hear far off the city clocks
Speaking of noonday drowsily ;
Lou crochets, Ann and Sarah knit,
And deep asleep the sooty flocks
Lie round the hawthorn roots like rocks.

Like a green wave the shade o'erwhelms
Their converse and their housewifery,
Like darting fish the sparrows flit ;
The babes stare upwards from their prams
With eyes as senseless-bright as gems.

Full fathom five, among the rocks,
Mermaids, sea-cloistered virgins, sit.

WINTER MOON

Tycho, a mountain in the moon,
Has long ago put out his fires—
Or so astronomers avow—
And dark the crater, and cold, yet now
About my hand, about the quires
Where this night through my hand has strewn
Words unavailing, frustrate phrases,
Tycho's malignant bale-fire blazes.

A licking frost, a lambent chill,
It lights the unkindled sacrifice
And plays about me to benumb.
The words I wait for will not come,
And cowering down, as under ice
Dumb water cowers, my lost thought still
Shows me a tree upon the wold,
That stands, and cracks its heart for cold.

NARCISSUS

' Narcissus !   Beautiful white narcissus ! '
Morning and evening as I go by
I hear the man at the corner cry :
' Narcissus !   Beautiful white narcissus ! '

A peck of March dust blows over his basket,
The papery blossoms are nipped and dry.
As well throw money away as buy
Pavement stuff that is drooping already.

This street is used by practical people,
They jostle onward, and so do I.
But if by chance a poet went by
I think he might stop, and give the man sixpence—

Not for the flowers ; for the dream's sake merely,
For the clear stream and the far sky,
And beauty lingering in the cry—
' Narcissus !   Beautiful white Narcissus ! '

THE RECORD

On winter eves when you are grown
Tired of your household talk of this
Gone well and t'other gone amiss
You will put on the gramophone.

Then shall the faithful air remit
My singing self which now I must
Engrave on silence and entrust
To the unmemoried ; then, quit

Of all but that one being, I
Shall bear your leaning souls along
Till voice and purport, songster and song,
Are fused into a single cry,

And you shall feel the authentic pang :
The traveller, pausing at the sound,
To see your listening looks around
Would think a living woman sang.

Quadruped on a bough,
Cat absolute, Cat behind
All cat-shows of your kind,
I see and salute you now :

Massive, tenacious, bland,
Sardonically surefoot,
Pacing along the sooty
Aspen branch, and fanned

By all the obsequious Spring
To ear fine-furred and strong
Squat nose conveys of song
Or scent wave-offering ;

As pace in stealthy hope
Through incense cloud and *Tu*
Es Petrus hullabaloo
Cardinals into Pope.

But more compactly wise,
More serpentine in sin
(My more than Mazarin)
Your commerce with the skies ;

While vacant and serene
Your eyes look down on me,
In all the wavering tree
The one unshaken green.

THE MAIDEN

IF I were to give you
A knot of white violets,
Plucked from their nest
Beneath the warm hedgerow,
To wear on your breast,
You would shake your head and sigh
To think the poor blossoms must wither and die.

If I were to give you
A cage of sweet singing-birds,
In a cruel hour
Betrayed from the greenwood,
To hang in your bower,
You would bid them all fly free,
So sad to your ear would their meek music be.

But if I were to give you
The heart out of my bosom,
At your least whim
With joy to burn ruddy,
With anguish to dim,
O then you wouldn't say no,
But take it, and use it, and never let it go.

THE POSSESSION

Now sinks the winter moon,
And brightens as she goes,
And on the village street
A shadow throws :

The shadow of the house
Wherein I darkling sit
Watching that other house
That stands opposite.

There she, towards whom my mind,
My senses, and my will,
Like a compass-needle fixed,
Point trembling still ;

She, towards whom the hushed
Tide of my blood is bound,
Lies in her maiden sleep,
Scornful and sound.

Wake not, reck not ;
Sleep warm and smoothly dream
How your shut window-pane
Looks back a gleam

Which splinters in my sight
As merciless as they—
Those diamond looks of scorn
You brandish by day.

Wake not, reck not
My wealth of love can hire
The cold-blood moon herself
To abet my desire ;

Nor how as I sit here,
Darkling within my shade,
Like some cool strategist
Whose plans are laid,

I watch my force advanced,
The unstirring shadow thrust
By her conniving hand
Over the ice-crust

Of the road, and up the wall
Until your window is won,
And from long watching I
And the shadow are one.

Then wake, then reckon,
Then hide your eyes for dread,
And know that more than shadow
Stands over your bed.

KIND FORTUNE

WHITE hand in brown hand lay,
To ears where brilliants shone
Hoarse voice went mumbling on
Till White Hand turned away :

' Husband handsome and kind
And pretty babes and gold
To squander—I 've been told
That story times out of mind !

' Good mother, be your next
Client some nursery-maid ;
You 'll drive a better trade
With such.'   ' Ah, don't be vexed,

' Lady ! I but declare
What is so smoothly writ
On this smooth palm.   Come, sit
By me again, compare

' Our two hands side by side,
Till like unlike thus grooved
So deep in mine has proved
To you I have not lied.

68

' Here is a husband, too,
And handsome, but not kind ;
Here, pretty babes, that pined
A weeping winter through

' Because I had nor gold
Nor pence their wants to heal,
And was too weak to steal ;
And here, down this long fold

' Of flesh, a life too long,
Frayed out with cares and crossed
With Lost, Lost, Lost . . .
Dearie, don't judge me wrong !

' Though outcast I and banned,
This once I have spoke true ;
And many would envy you
What 's in this happy hand.'

EVENSONG IN WINTER

A RED light streams from windows and doors,
The flagstones clack and the organ roars,
And through the churchyard, silent and glum,
Figures darker than darkness come ;
And a child says : ' Mother, I can tell !
It 's the Devils trooping out of Hell.'

SELF HEAL

FIRST at our meeting-place
As I practised patience
A flower looked out of the hedge
As though seeking acquaintance ;
And I thought, when my dear one came
She should tell me its name.

For she boasted, there grew not a herb
In heath, meadow, or wood
That she couldn't clap name to as pat
As old Culpeper could ;
And rather than own herself spent,
Why, a name she 'd invent.

Many a time since then,
And in many a shire,
Has that flower looked up at me
As if to enquire :
Have you learned me yet ? and below
My breath I say : No !

For my dear one but came to declare
That while scorning to flirt
A new love was more to her mind ;
At the time I was hurt ;
But I think (though the song it may mar)
Things are best as they are.

OUT of the field two hoers raise
Their heads to watch the express go past,
And swift think I :
How stablished and secure their days,
But mine flit by too fast.

The lolling vapour thins away,
The air is sweet and silent again,
And they think slow :
Ah, to what happiness speed they,
The folk who go by train !

THE MILL IN THE VALLEY

Though for ten years and more the mill
Disused and tenantless has been,
A grey house and a hanging green
Dwell steadfast in their mirror still.

Where erst were waggons bringing wheat,
Were trampling hooves, were whistling boys,
The water with an idle voice
Goes brimming idly through the leat.

The roof is falling in, the door
Upon its crazy hinges grieves ;
West winds autumnal drift the leaves
Over the empty granary floor ;

And from all life it is estranged,
Unless a stranger come this way,
To lean upon the gate, and say :
' 'Twas busy once, but times are changed.'

The miller was a careful man,
Thrifty and keen, a man of weight ;
But thrift 's a grass-work against fate,
And in his time the change began :

Until for waggons ten that crossed
His bridge there came but five, but two,
And he had nothing left to do
But close the mill, for all was lost.

To shun it ruined, once his boast,
He to a distant town did fare ;
There, died ; but thence the man of care
Returned anon a careless ghost.

Through the long winter-time he keeps
His comfortable grave, but when
The April dusks stretch out again,
When hawking swallow dips, and leaps

The fish all silver from a spool
Of spreading silver spreading still,
That sets the grey house and green hill
Rocking and deepening through the pool,

He comes—not now as once he trod,
Ownerly and deliberate,
But sauntering at a holiday gait ;
And pauses to set up his rod

And knots the fly and having essayed
A whip or two creeps crafty near
The water's edge, as though the fear
That he, a shadow, should cast a shade

Were the one care he had in mind :
The very stones of his house-place
Cry out to him his old disgrace,
But he is deaf to them, and blind.

Others have seen him plain, but I
Him thus revisiting have traced
But by the surface silver-laced
Where the flung line has fallen awry,

Or when the chatter of the reel
Discovers at a cast well-sped
The millpond giving up its dead
Duly to the dead master's creel.

AWAKE FOR LOVE

They are all gone to bed ;
But I for love of them am still awake,
Companioning the fire that falls a-drowse ;
My spirit walks around the darkened house,
And feels the wind, and sees the heavens shake
Their diamond tresses overhead.

Love has extended it
Into the changing stature of a cloud ;
My arms embrace the eaves, my bosom pressed
To the cold slates yearns warm above their rest,
Over their roof-tree my vast love is bowed,
As bowed before their hearth I sit.

My wakefulness includes
Their sleep, my compact kept with time and space
Vouches for them enfranchised, their dreams glide
Unchallenged through my being, as the tide
Of guarded life-blood on with even pace
Flows through the body's solitudes.

TOO EARLY SPRING

Has but half a day, or is half a year
Gone by since to these rounded meadows and shy
Entangled willow copses I came with my dear?

Leaves were crowding prick-eared to the live air . . .
But when? That small red sun bewinters us again,
And round us the trees stand motionless and bare.

Come, let 's away, my dear, let 's away without noise.
Our Spring has stolen hence, and why do we linger
On this last year's grass? Ah, where are all our joys?

DEATH THE BRIDEGROOM

O Bride, why dost thou delay ?
The Bridegroom waits, it is thy wedding day.
Now, while the sun has yet a stair to climb,
Now, while thy beauty yet foretells its prime,
 Arise, and come away !
 Yet a while, said she.
 Wedded I would not be
Till I have trimmed my virgin coronet
With windflower, stitchwort, and white violet.
Once more a-blossoming let me go !
On my behalf the flowering roots were set,
And well, well do I know
Whereabouts in my Father's park they grow.

O Bride, why dost thou delay ?
The Bridegroom waits, it is thy wedding day.
Now, while the sun his noonday splendour wields
Nor yet with lengthening shadow scythes the fields,
 Arise, and come away !
 Yet a while, said she.
 Wedded I cannot be
Till I have packed my bridal dower-box
With ermine, emeralds, gold, and the meek flocks

Of threaded pearls, and then fastened on
My cloak that 's damasked like July hollyhocks—
For now Spring tints look wan,
And Summer's are the colours I would don.

O Bride, why dost thou delay ?
Morning and summer both are fled away,
And now it is thy wedding night,
And out of the black sky the snow falls white.
  No longer mayest thou delay.
  Yet a while, said she.
  Though wedded I must be,
Suffer me yet to warm my hands before
The fire, old love-letters to read o'er,
And have one last look round ;
Ay, and beneath God's rood I would implore
That mercy may abound,
For perilous is the journey whereon we are bound.

PAY WHAT THOU OWEST

SEVEN loud and lusty bells
Hang in our steeple ;
Ancient they are, so Parson tells,
And have names like people :

Francis Philpot, Brother John,
Wenceslas Carey,
Bristol, Kirry Leison
And Gaudy Mary.

All have names save only one,
Deepest and slowest,
Him the ringers in their fun
Call Pay What Thou Owest ;

All ring true save him alone,
Flawed in the casting,
Harsh and dull has been his tone
From everlasting.

Twice a week on winter nights
The ringers assemble,
Practising triples and such-like flights
Till the air 's a-tremble.

Fleet and clear the echoes scud
From rafter to rafter,
And Pay What Thou Owest with a thud
Follows halting after.

The other bells so smooth of speech
Answer each other,
Sweetly answering each to each
Like sister and brother ;

They laugh as merrily as elves,
Seeming to flout him ;
You 'd fancy they said amongst themselves :
' We could do without him.'

And when as a school-boy I for a while
Was feeling down-hearted
I 've sat at the dark end of the aisle
Till the tears have started

To think that I and that bell alike
Were both unneeded ;
Yes, and I 've groaned aloud belike,
As harshly as he did.

Old year out and new year in—
Time 's a rare songster,
And a man doesn't care as he sits at the inn
How he felt as a youngster.

81

A child in the cradle, a friend in the grave,
Getting and spending,
With the bells coming in at the end of the stave
Like a tol-de-rol ending ;

Merry come sad and even come odd—
If you 've an ear for
That song you don't stop to ask your God :
' What am I here for ? '

Man on earth and bells on the wind—
Often I 've said it—
Clash the same pattern time out of mind
To their Maker's credit ;

Only the bells had this to boast ;
They lasted longer :
' Here 's the Long-Livers ! ' I called as a toast—
It seems I was wrong there.

For Pay What Thou Owest is cracked at last,
A crack that will flourish
Up through his singing side as fast
As this sore I nourish ;

So it 's a match between him and me :
I think he will win it,
For to run a noose from the bough of a tree
Is the work of a minute.

He to the foundry and I to clay—
Since we must sever,
One debt standing over I 'd have him pay
Ere he 's dumbed for ever :

Gaudy Mary and the rest
They can be merry all,
But Pay What Thou Owest is the best
When it comes to a burial.

THE VISIT

Last night it chanced that I, who dwell alone,
And am not much dismayed
To hear my solitary midnight said,
Nor wish for livelier company than my own,
Hearing the hour
Spelled slowly stroke by stroke from the church tower,

And gathering up myself for bed, my mind
Prepared to disarray
Itself of yet another dullish day
Yet somewhat pitying that which it resigned,
Became aware
Of a sigh, not my own, breathed on the air.

' You have guessed right,' said she. ' I am a ghost.
I will not haunt you long ;
But I am weary, for the wind blows strong,
And looking in on you, you seemed almost
One such as I ;
So I am come to bear you company.'

Right neighbourly beside my hearth she sat,
Full fluently conversed,
As one in England's decent topics versed—
Birds, beasts, the Royal Family, this and that ;

84

But nothing told
Me of the dead, save that they feel the cold.

At length all things seemed said.   A silence fell,
And in that silence we heard,
Loud as a trumpeter, a chirping bird
Greet the March morning ; then quoth I : ' Well, well—
The days begin
To draw—'   ' O no,' cried she.   ' The nights draw in ! '

SPARROW HALL

' WHO lives in that house,
That is so old and grey,
Like a sleepy old nurse
Who at close of day
Sits watching with kind eyes
Children at their play ?

' For frolicking in the wind
Blossom lilac and may,
Laburnum and guelder rose,
Tossing this way and that way ;
And the young-voiced blackbirds
Sing on the blossomed spray.'

' No one lives there at all.
Ever since my day
The trees have bloomed untended,
Whilst wandering into decay
The house sleeps in their midst :
I have never heard say

' That ghost walked there,
Good men to affray.
It 's a pity nobody takes it.

Perhaps, Sir, you may ?
For standing so long empty
The rent would be little to pay.'

' No, friend ; it is not for me ;
I must hold on my way,
For life calls me, and love calls me,
And I must obey.
Perhaps I shall come back to it
When I am old and grey.'

THE DECOY

In these level fields
That still remember the sea
I have hollowed a creek,
I have planted a grove ;
I have bidden the proud
Air-wandering birds that rove
Day-long from cloud to cloud
To shelter in me.

And I have tamed two birds,
Called Metre and Rhyme,
At whose sweet calling
All thoughts may be beguiled
To my preparèd place ;
Yet tamed, by blood they are wild,
Being on all-mothering Space
Begotten by Time.

DATE DUE

GAYLORD   PRINTED IN U.S.A.